Tommy,

Your an amazing Brother in law – More like just a brother. You've always been so good to me. I Love you

"Mindi"
Melinda L. Moreland

Cherish ME

by

Melinda L. Moreland

© 2002 by Melinda L. Moreland. All rights reserved.
No part of this book may be reproduced, stored in a retrieval system, or transmitted by any means, electronic, mechanical, photocopying, recording, or otherwise, without written permission from the author.

ISBN: 1-4033-3545-1 (e-book)
ISBN: 1-4033-3546-X (Paperback)
ISBN: 1-4033-3547-8 (Dustjacket)

Library of Congress Control Number: 2002092176

This book is printed on acid free paper.

Printed in the United State of America
Bloomington, IN

1st Books - rev. 08/13/02

DEDICATION

I Would like to dedicate Cherish ME to Jesus first: for without you I would be nothing, Yet with you I can do all things.

My Husband Roy, My Children Joseph and Dawna, My Parents Ernest and Donna Montoya, Grandma Jeanette Tomlinson, Uncle Lee and Aunt Geneva, Bill and Maggie Hurd, My sister Kim, My Friends Chyrel, Deb, Becky, Lisa, Melissa and Virginia.

Last but yet so important my Pastor and his wife, Pastor Steven J. and Donna Salazar. With out each of you none of this would have been possible.

Thank you so much for believing in me and your love. Mindi

A HEARTFELT PRAYER

Something so simple,
yet from my heart.
On this day,
I give you God's art.
Upon my heart these words were put.
To share with one,
to share with all.
They're all written so simple
yet all so true.
They speak of his love,
and his coming too.
In Heaven each time one is read,
a tear comes to His eyes.
For He knows the word has been heard
from here to nigh
of how He died
yet how He LIVES.
So if the words through God's love I've wrote
has touched a heart.
Then, thank you, Lord.
I've done my part.

Inspired By God
Melinda L. Moreland

Dedicated to Uncle Lee & Aunt Geneva

Melinda L. Moreland

THE PRAYER

In despair, I cried,
so lost in my own pain,
I forgot to look towards God.
I forgot He always holds my hand.

Then, in shame I cried;
I closed my eyes, and prayed
this prayer.

LORD help me be what I should be.
Touch my life and help me heal.
Let me not live with anger and hurt,
but teach me to strive for love and understanding.
Help me, LORD, to trust in You and You alone.
Be with me, LORD, each and every day,
and help me lead others in the right way.

I praised the LORD as the last teardrop fell.
I just knew that all would be well.

He touched my life,
and he'll touch yours.
Just trust in Him forever more,
and in the end you will see the
Streets of Gold
along with me.

Inspired By God
Melinda l. Moreland

WILL YOU GO

The day has come,
all hope is here,
and fear will be no more.

We cry sweet tears,
we laugh with joy,
we raise our hands,
and praise our Lord.

The trumpet sounds,
the angels appear,
and we know for sure that
our Jesus is near.

Some are happy,
some are sad,
some don't understand,
and that's too bad.

No more tears,
no more sorrows,
the Heavens open.
We laugh with joy
we're homeward bound.

Some will go,
Some will stay,
For it is our Blessed Judgement Day.

WILL YOU GO?

Inspired By God
Melinda L. Moreland

Melinda L. Moreland

BELIEVE

You feel the tingle
of the Spirit.
Yet you ignore.

You feel the rush
of Angel Wings.
Yet you doubt.

You feel My Presence,
Yet you wonder
if I'm real.

I've held you
I've cradled you
I've walked with you
I've carried you.

Now Believe
I AM!

Inspired By God
Melinda L. Moreland

FOR YOU

All alone she sat and cried,
she thought.

He watched with despair
as he lost all he had,
he thought.

But wait!
She felt the brush of His hand.
She knew.

But wait!
He felt the spirit of the Lord with him.
He knew.

I'm with you.
I never left you.
Reach out and touch Me.
I'm here!

FOR YOU

Inspired By God
Melinda L. Moreland

Melinda L. Moreland

I'M HERE

I lit the sun,
I hung the stars,
I colored the grass,
and I created you!

I parted the sea,
I wrote the commandments,
and all you had to do was just believe
In Me.

I walked on earth,
I cured the sick,
and I taught you about
My Love.

I hung on the cross,
I died for your sins,
But yet
I LIVE!

Believe what is in front of you.
Touch me for I am real!
I feel your pain.
I hear your cries.
I know your doubts.

Come to Me,
Come to Me,
It's so simple,
I'm Here

Inspired By God
Melinda l. Moreland

Cherish ME

ONE TEARDROP TOO MANY

I see the teardrops falling
I hear the softly spoken prayer
I know sometimes you cannot feel Me
But I promise I am there.

I felt the pain you felt today
I know that you were hurt
I held you when you cried
I wanted to heal your hurt.

Today I watched you walking along that mountain path
I watched you crying once again
I thought how very sad
for all you'd have to do is reach out and take My hand.

Through all the years
I've watched you suffer
I've watched you cry
I've watched you die
please let me help you
at least let Me try
Because you've cried one teardrop too many.

Inspired By God
Melinda L. Moreland

Dedicated to My Cousin Jeannie.

Melinda L. Moreland

THE DREAM

I dreamed I was walking
up this rocky path.
I kept stumbling and falling.
I couldn't find the right direction to go
each path looking worse than the last.
I would cry out, God, help me,
but it would seem to no avail.
I felt lost and alone
wondering if there was any way
I could reach the top.
I was so lost in my own
pain and anguish
I could not feel His Presence
yet I continued to struggle on.
As I reached the top
I had a sense of such sweet peace
because even though I had stumbled many times
I had done good and God was pleased.
I realized then
God never leaves us
He was there all the time
mending my wounds
healing my heart
helping me up when I stumbled.
and He's here now.

Inspired By God
Melinda L. Moreland
February 23, 1999

I LOVE YOU

I'm standing on a cliff
I can hear the waves
hitting the rocks.

I feel the wind
whipping through my hair.

The spray of salt water
mingles with my tears.

I've Lost…

Jump

Is what the sounds say.

I step from the cliff
I should fall,
but a hand holds me
I hear a voice say
all is not lost.
I LOVE YOU!!

Inspired By God
Melinda L. Moreland
February 23, 1999

Melinda L. Moreland

WONDER

Last night as I lay sleeping
a dream disturbed my rest.
It was a storm that rivaled all the rest.
I saw the clouds begin to gather.
I felt the rain begin to fall.
I heard the thunder start to rumble.
But in the midst of it all,
I saw our Lord just standing there,
and in his eyes I saw the pain.

He touched His heart and blew the clouds,
and then the SON appeared.
At His bosom the children rested,
In His arms so tightly they were held.

Now you've been left behind to weep and wonder,
at the sorrow of the day.
For tomorrow is not set in stone,
and it may not be the life you know
upon the rising sun,
but eternity's light that you see.

Don't take the chance that you've got time
to make it right with God.
Just take the step right now to stand.
Before the Lord you see…

Inspired By God
Melinda L. Moreland
April 21, 1999

PEACE

High atop a mountain,
looking down upon the valley low.
I sat in awesome wonder,
and thought of days not long ago.
When in my haste to reach the top,
the bottom seemed as far as I could go.

I cried for strength from God above.
My eye's I set on Him,
but like many on this journey
that seemed to have no end.
I sometimes faltered on my path,
and had to start again.
So with my knee's bloodied from the falls
I seemed to take each day.

I reached above and took His hand,
and gave to Him my life complete.
Somehow through His gracious love
I found the strength to climb,
and now today my rest is sweet.
For in His bosom I now sleep.

Inspired By God
Melinda L. Moreland
August 4th 1999

Melinda L. Moreland

PREPARE

I walked this earth,
I healed you, sick
in body and in mind,
with just a promise of My love.
"I AM COMING"

I carry your burden's
I wipe your tears away
I hold you in the darkest hours
until this day.
" I AM COMING"

I gave My life
on a cross at Calvary
to buy the pardon of your sins
for this day to come.
"I AM COMING"

Prepare your hearts
Prepare your souls
Prepare your Children
Tell everyone that you know
It's time to go.
"I AM COMING"

The day draws nigh
when you shall join Me in the sky
and to heaven We shall rise.
"I AM COMING"

Inspired By God
Melinda L. Moreland
August 18, 1999

BEGINNING

Somewhere in the soft night
a child was born.
No castle was about
just a stable and a manager
to hold Him through the night.

Somewhere in the dark night
In a garden He sat.
Speaking softly to the Father
of what was to come upon the light.

One morning with the SON so bright
He carried our cross to Calvary
Where He Hung.

Sins forgiven
LIFE BEGUN!!!!!

Inspired By God
Melinda L. Moreland
August 26,1999

Melinda L. Moreland

TAKE THE TIME

I have spoken of My coming
many times before.

I have freely given of My love,
to the weary laden and more.

I have given comfort on a dark night
to the lost and all alone.

I have given forgiveness without remembrance
to all who have asked.

I have given a million lifetimes
to this world.
Now that time is closing fast.

Now to each of you I ask,

Give to those whose souls are lost.

Spread My word to each
who is in need.

Help Me touch each heart that is hurt..

So take that minute
don't let it pass
just introduce Me
so My love can
fill the gap.

Inspired By God
Melinda L. Moreland
September 10, 1999

GOD'S LOVE

Each morning as I rise
to speak with God above,
I look around in awesome wonder
at the beauty of God's love.

You can't help but see God's love
as the sun comes alive,
shadowing the mountains
In the soft outline of light.

You have to stop and wonder
as the dawn begins again,
at what our Lord must have thought
as he watched the first sunrise begin.

Each day begins the same for us,
with the sun upon the peaks,
Casting brilliant light upon the ones
you love still fast asleep.

So, stop right now and say a prayer
for those who do not see.

For a day is coming soon
when a different SON you'll see.
On those mountain peaks He'll stand,
arms spread in love,
Welcoming His children home,
To Heaven up above.

Inspired By God
Melinda L. Moreland
September 12, 1999

Melinda L. Moreland

SUFFER THE LITTLE CHILDREN

Many years ago in my darkest hour,
I'd hide beneath my teddy bear
for what seemed to be like hours.
I'd pray to God to keep me safe
and not let the day begin.

Yet in the cool dampness of the dawn
the day would always start again.
I could hear the floor creak
from the footsteps in the hall.
I'd pray a silent prayer to God
to please help me build a wall.

Yet those footsteps seemed to never stop
until they reached the fear buried deep
inside my heart.

As a child I always thought
God never heard my prayers.
I didn't think He loved me.
I didn't think He cared.

It took years of pain and anguish
for me to see the light.
God's love is sufficient,
It was that love and is that love
that carries me through each night.

Now each day when a trouble comes about
On this simple truth I stand!!!!

God has no control
upon a man whose soul is lost.
Yet if to him you give your heart,
He'll be standing there beside you

Cherish ME

until Heaven we do depart.

Inspired By God
Melinda L. Moreland
September 16, 1999

Melinda L. Moreland

ARE YOU

Are you
Lost and alone
seeking a friend to call your own?

Are you,
hiding from the outside world
to afraid to venture out?

Are you,
A small child crying from fear
in the dark night
wanting the loving comfort of a
Mother's arms?

Are you,
A woman standing in a quite house
your heart gone, maybe lost forever
wanting the comfort you think only
his touch can bring?

Are you,
A man standing on a mountain side
watching the sun go down
crying out for someone, anyone
to notice you're alive?

Are you,
Looking for someone to calm your fears
heal your heart, and fill every void?

There's only one healer for the heart.
There's only one who can comfort the soul.

IT'S JESUS
Just take his hand

Cherish ME

and give him control.

Inspired By God
Melinda L. Moreland
October 7, 1999

Melinda L. Moreland

HE CAN

So lost and alone
no one to turn to,
no place to call your own.

Looking in the dark corners
searching always,
but never finding what seems to be lost.

Worrying over what tomorrow holds,
crying over yesterday.
Striving to reach the light at the end of the tunnel.
Never turning to the light in your heart.

Fighting and struggling yet never
giving in.Knowing He's out there,
Yet never stopping to let Him in.

He's been there all the time
lingering softly in your mind.
Waiting for you to give Him
just a moment of your time.

He can take the broken hearted,
and mend their broken wings.

He can take the broken spirited,
and give them life beyond their dreams.

He can do anything
see the sun, the stars, the sky.

He's there in your heart
Just ask!!!
Just try!!!

Cherish ME

Inspired By God
Melinda L. Moreland
October 22nd, 1999

Melinda L. Moreland

OK LORD

Here I'm standing
not understanding
wanting to know
what tomorrow might hold.

Show me Lord,
what's on your mind
for each step I take
through this humble life of mine.

Teach me Lord,
to take a breath
and give you time
to walk me up each
mountain side.

Help me Lord,
to find the joy
I feel I've Lost
Yet know You have.

Here I am Lord,
humbly at your feet
at last!!

Inspired By God
Melinda L. Moreland
October 22, 1999

HERE I STAND

Here it is GOD
I give it to you
the hurt in my heart
the fear in my soul.

to you I am learning
to turn with every
worry and concern.

At your feet LORD
help me to lay
each problem of my day.

Even if through a
heartache sometimes
I may pray.

So take me LORD
just as I am
crying at your throne
lost and alone.

Inspired By God
Melinda L. Moreland
October 22, 1999

Melinda L. Moreland

STEP FROM THE BOAT

I want you to stop talking,
and start walking.
STEP FROM THE BOAT.

I want it left at the throne,
left untouched for Me alone.
STEP FROM THE BOAT.

Have faith in My word
stand on it firm.
STEP FROM THE BOAT.

I've called you for Me
not for man, but for Me.
STEP FROM THE BOAT.

I am the Healer.
I am the Savior.
I am the one who sets you free.
STEP FROM THE BOAT.

I walk on water.
Come walk with Me.
STEP FROM THE BOAT.

Inspired By God
Melinda L. Moreland
October 25, 1999

Dedicated to My Friend Becky Dixon

HANNAH ANGEL*

Hannah Angel
Sent from Heaven
on an Angels wing .
Bright as the sun
soft as the night.
Gentle and kind *
loved and cherished
for all time.
A gift from above
to a world so lost.
An angel was sent.
A gift of love,
A gift of life.

Hannah Angel.

Inspired By God
Melinda L. Moreland
Oct. 29th, 1999

Dedicated to Hannah Montoya

Melinda L. Moreland

HE'S THERE

Lost in a heartache,
trapped in despair,
holding your hand.
He's There!!!

Tear's gently falling,
our heart's open wide.
He's There!!!

Even in heartbreak,
when there seems
to be no day break,
He's There!!!

Softly in prayer
as He crosses your heart,
Just know.
He's there.

Inspired By God
Melinda L Moreland
October 31, 1999

Cherish ME

SOMETHING SO SIMPLE

A simple smile
A touch in kind
A love so special
It seems to be just mine.

A soft morning breeze
A salt water spray from the sea
A touch so comforting
It can only come from a King.

A blade of grass
a snowflake drifting
In the air so light
A sun so bright
Yet it cannot compare
To a SON on a Cross
for our sins to spare.

Inspired By God
Melinda L. Moreland
November 29, 1999

Melinda L. Moreland

NOT EVEN A THOUGHT

A moment in time
A love so divine
His life given for yours and mine.

Not a moment was taken
when he did think
to ask in wonder,
or even question why.

He gave His life
without a thought of
Himself.

Just the laughter of a child
whose life through His love
Has been made right.

Inspired by God
Melinda L. Moreland
March 15, 2000

SPECIAL MOMENTS

Special moments of
days gone past.
Cherished childhood memories
of a love that will always last.
A brother lost, but not gone.
A moment without him,
but not for long.

A tear you shed upon that day,
for a goodbye
seemed to be your fate.

Yet Jesus stands here
now to say.
that to your brother
hello is all you'll say.
When through heaven's gate
you walk that day.

Inspired By God
Melinda L Moreland
June 27, 2000

Dedicated : my friend Chyrel Doyon Rue

Melinda L. Moreland

DEAR GOD

What have we become
when we hate, because of the
color of someone.
When we care not that somewhere
a heartache has begun.
When we cannot feel the hurt
from someone that we love.
When we can no longer touch a stranger with kindness
or in love.
When our hearts have lost the laughter from your SON
shining up above
When it seems we're reaching to touch you,
and feel your love.
Dear God what have we become?
LOST!!!!

TURN TO HIM

Inspired By God
Melinda L. Moreland
June 27th, 2000

Cherish ME

JUST LISTEN

I walked this earth so long ago
A man just like yourself,
to tell you all of God above!
SOME LISTENED
I walked the long and lonely walk
all alone with a cross upon my back
to free you from your sins!
SOME LISTENED
I walk with you now, each and
everyday .
Until the day when unto you
I shall return.
PLEASE LISTEN
What will it take?
What must this world so awful deal you,
for your heart to turn to ME?
PLEASE LISTEN
Before your time has come too late.
JUST LISTEN

INSPIRED BY GOD
MELINDA MORELAND
OCTOBER 8TH 2000

Melinda L. Moreland

WALK WITH ME

I've stood here many times
before asking you to take My
hand, and let Me lead you through the valley low.
Yet you want to go alone.
Please walk with Me.

The rain begins to fall
the thunder seems loud to all who can hear.
yet in the shadow of My love
the storm is calm.
Come walk with Me.

The time is coming
for this old world to be no more.
When all that is asleep
shall rise to be with Me.
Just take that final step My child.

WALK WITH ME!!!

Inspired By God
Melinda l. Moreland
October 9th, 2000

THE TIME HAS COME
FOLLOW ME

The time has come
to take a stand
Just take My hand -
Follow me.

The time has come
for you to lay
all earthly things aside
Just take My hand -
Follow Me.

The time has come
for you to join
the chosen one's
Just take My hand -
Follow Me.

The time has come
for all the dead in
Christ to rise; for you to meet
Me in the sky
Just take My hand
Follow Me.

Inspired By God
Mark 2 :14
Melinda L. Moreland
October 12, 2000

Melinda L. Moreland

THE CHILD

The child inside has
been set free
to be the child of God
you were meant to be.

Tonight you died
a death so sweet,
but a life in Me
has just begun.
A life of one.

Just breathe Me in
Just live through Me
Just be Me
through Me
My child.
*I AM!!!

Inspired By God
Melinda L Moreland
October 12, 2000

I AM SPEAKING

Softly spoken prayers
filling a room full of saints.
And Me

I am here to touch your hearts
to heal the hurts
and mend your broken spirits.
I'm Here

Reach out your hands
bow down on your knee's
Praise Me
Live in Me.
I AM

Inspired By God
Melinda L. Moreland
October 15th of 2000

Melinda L. Moreland

AS IT SHOULD BE

I spoke to you,
and you listened.
AS IT SHOULD BE!

I touched you,
and you reached forward
and took My hand.
AS IT SHOULD BE!

You opened your heart,
when at your door
I Knocked.
AS IT SHOULD BE!

Now live through Me,
walk through Me,
speak through Me.
AS IT SHOULD BE!

Inspired By God
Melinda L. Moreland
October 15th, 2000

Cherish ME

JUST AS

Just as
the seasons change
so must you.

Just as
the day turns to night
turn to Me.

Just as
a child your faith
in Me should be.

I am the answer
you seek to all things.

Just as it is written
JUST AS IT SHOULD BE!!!!

Inspired By God
Melinda L. Moreland
October 17th, 2000

Melinda L. Moreland

COME LIVE WITH ME

Have you ever
stopped and looked
at the color of the tree's?
I MADE THEM!!

Have you ever
looked at babies
all soft and cuddly?
I MADE THEM!!!

Have you ever
longed for peace
and heartache no more,
Street's of gold
and mansions on high?
I Made them for you!!

COME LIVE WITH ME
IT'S YOUR CHOICE!

Inspired By God
Melinda L. Moreland
October 21, 2000

Cherish ME

MAKE THE CHOICE

I sent My SON
to earth to die on
a cross for all
My wayward children.
WAS IT IN VAIN?

I sent the Holy Spirit
to comfort your souls,
and lead you to Me.
YET YOU IGNORE!

A time is coming
when My Son shall return.
Will you meet Him in the sky
or be left behind to wonder?

I have given you the
key's to the kingdom.
Open the door.
Before tomorrow is no more
and Hell is your only reward!

MAKE THE CHOICE!!!

Inspired By God
Melinda L. Moreland
October 21, 2000

Melinda L. Moreland

ALL I AM

I've had many friends
in this life of mine.
Cherished ones, loved ones, and lost ones.
Yet You are the best one.

I've been down many roads
that went no where.
Yet always ended in
Your loving arms.

I've had heartache's
I thought would never end,
and I've laughed till I cried with joy.
Yet no matter what,
You were there.

You've laughed with me,
cried with me, and
stayed with me when all
seemed lost.
You've never failed me
no matter what

So I give you all I have left.
ALL OF ME!!
I LOVE YOU LORD.

Inspired By God
Melinda L. Moreland
October 21, 2000

GO ALL THE WAY

Don't believe the doubters
of the world,
who believe getting half way to
God is all it will take.
Go All the Way.
Stand on faith,
Stand on Me.

Don't read part of my word
and find your answers.
Read it all.
Go All the Way.
Walk in faith.
Walk with me.

Some time's it may not
be easy to step out on faith.
Yet I am asking you to do just that.
Go All the Way.
Live in faith
Live in me.

I have all the answers
Just follow me,
for the mysteries of heaven
are yours to see.
Just put your hand in Mine.
Trust in faith,
Trust in Me.
Come go all the way to Heaven with Me.

Inspired By God
Melinda L. Moreland
October 22, 2000

Melinda L. Moreland

TURN TO ME

Outside the storm has begun
so violent with no control.
Inside your soul a storm is raging,
a heart not sure where to turn
for shelter.
TURN TO ME..

Inside the house so dark
from despair.
On your knees you must
bend to give a soul
so lost to Him.
TURN TO ME..

To My people searching
for answers, in a
world that is fading fast.
TURN TO ME..
BEFORE TOMORROW IS NO MORE
TURN TO ME

Inspired By God
Melinda L. Moreland
October 22, 2000

Cherish ME

THAT'S WHO JESUS IS

An old cuddly teddy bear.
The petals of a rose.
A baby cooing in it's bed.
That's what Jesus is and more.

A tender touch, a loving smile.
The laughter of a child.
Sunlight shining through snowflakes.
That's what Jesus is and more.

The soft fur of a newborn kitten.
A husband saying I Love You.
A Mom who never gives up.
That's what Jesus is and more.

A King,
Who gave His life
for you and I.
That's Who Jesus Is.

Inspired By God
Melinda L. Moreland
October 24, 2000

Melinda L. Moreland

JUST LET JESUS

All the wonders of the world
at our feet have been laid.
Just let Jesus show you the way.

We have the authority
for miracles to behold.
Through His word it is told.
Just let Jesus show you the way.

This is not hard,
not a mystery I'm sure.
He's easily found when on
knees you do bow.
Just let Jesus show you the way.

Salvation is just a sincere heart,
and a prayer away.
Then to Heaven you are bound..
Just let Jesus show you the way.

Inspired By God
Melinda L. Moreland
October 24, 2000

Cherish ME

HOW JESUS MUST LOVE US

From Heaven He came,
to a world that was lost
To show His children of God's love
no matter the cost.
How Jesus must love us!!

On a Cross He did hang.
Surrounded by thieves,
He gave His life to set us free.
How Jesus must love us!!

Someday soon in the sky
He will come,
Welcoming His Children home
with arms open wide.
How Jesus must love us!!

HOW MUCH DO YOU LOVE HIM??

Inspired By God
Melinda L. Moreland
October 26, 2000

Melinda L. Moreland

TIME

Alarm clock ringing,
you're up like a shot
the day is beginning.
Yet to Him you gave not a thought.

Running and running,
losing your mind.
racing towards tomorrow
when today has not
yet been left behind.

This story is so sad,
but yet it is true.
We want Him around
when there's things
we need Him to do.

Yet not a second,
not a minute,
not a moment
do we have to give Him of our
precious time.

Oh how lucky we are
this day I must say
that Jesus had time
to hang on a cross
for your sins and mine

Inspired By God
Melinda L. Moreland
October 26, 2000

A LOVE GIVEN

A story of love
that will rival all time.

A love so true
your heart would
have to be blind.

He was a man
just like you and I.
Yet a King He is
to your soul and mine.

He has given His love,
Not to mention His life
for your sins,
for my sins.
To Him it just seemed right.

How sad for him
I'm sorry to say
He love's a nation
of people who are
lazy these days.

Yet with that in mind
His love is still true.
What will it take
for ours to be too.

Inspired By God
Melinda L, Moreland
October 27, 2000

Melinda L. Moreland

TOUCH A HEART

Take our broken heart
and mend them
unto you.

Take our broken spirits
and help us find
Your love anew.

This life we live,
so short its true,
means nothing, Lord
except for You.

Touch a heart.

Inspired by God
Melinda L. Moreland
October 29, 2000

JESUS IS COMING

I watch as the billowing clouds
roll in over the peaks
of the mountains.
I look for the SON!

I stand in a field of daisies
listening to the birds sing.
I look to the horizon
and listen for the
sound of the trumpet.

The SON is coming.
Of this I am sure.

Open your hearts.
Open your souls.
Look to the sky.
JESUS IS COMING!!!

Inspired By God
Melinda L. Moreland
October 30, 2000

Melinda L. Moreland

DO IT NOW

Enough is enough
I say to you now.
I've given you chances
upon chances to follow Me
DO IT NOW!

Enough is enough
come to me now
your time is short,
on your knees you must bow.
follow Me
DO IT NOW!

Enough is enough
of this world,
I can no longer ignore.
Follow Me
DO IT NOW!

The day is coming
I promise you this
when there will be
no more chances.
Follow Me.
DO IT NOW!

Inspired by God
Melinda L. Moreland
November 1, 2000

Cherish ME

IN DUE TIME

Today I may send My SON
to bring you home.
You know not,
Just I.

Tomorrow My SON
could shine bright
who really knows.
Just I

I t does not matter
what day He may come
If in your heart
He is the one.

Just let Him hold
all your tomorrow's.
Not a worry will you find,
Just Heaven..

IN DUE TIME

Inspired By God
Melinda L. Moreland
November 1, 2000

Melinda L. Moreland

WHAT WOULD YOU DO

What would you do
if the sun didn't shine
if the sky wasn't blue..

What would you do
if you woke with a start
to find there was no
one but you..

What would you do…
would you believe then
or still live in doubt?

What would you do
If Jesus came.
Would you go?
Would you stay?
If you're not sure
then I suggest
You pray!!

Inspired By God
Melinda L. Moreland
November 2, 2000

A MOTHERS PRAYER

Oh, Lord, sometimes
I fall so short
Of what I'm sure
You want a mother to be.

To me you have given
two special people
One boy,
One girl.

Yet sometimes
as their parent
I feel so inept.
Not sure which way to turn
Or what you think is best.

So here I am, Lord,
teach me
to be, through You.
The mother you
want me to be.
A mother in need.
A mother in deed.

Inspired By God
Melinda L. Moreland
November 3, 2000

Melinda L. Moreland

WHAT MORE DO YOU NEED

You wait for a miracle
to believe.
I created earth
what more do you need?

You look for a sign
to come to me.
I was born of a virgin.
What more do you need?

You wait and you look
to give your heart to Me.
I died on a cross for you.
What more do you need?

I am coming and coming soon.
Stop waiting and looking.
Just believe.
What more do you need?

Inspired By God
Melinda L. Moreland
November 6, 2000

JUST A MATTER OF TIME

It's just a matter
of time before time
is no more.

It's just a matter
of time before
the trumpet sounds.

It's just a matter
of time before
I split the eastern sky.

It's just a matter
of time before
it's all changed
in the twinkling of an eye.

It's just a matter
of time
Time for you to make a choice
before time as you know it
Is No More..

What's stopping you.
What's holding you back?
Its just a matter of time.

Inspired By God
Melinda L. Moreland
November 6, 2000

Melinda L. Moreland

HOME TIME

To give His life
for you and I.
What a sacrifice
for all man kind.

A love for His
Children,
not forsaken,
just given,
for all time.

A tear in your eye,
a love so divine.
let Him touch
your heart.
It's almost home time.

Inspired By God
Melinda L. Moreland
November 7, 2000

FOR ALL TIME

My soul I've given to you my Lord.
I promise not a moment
not a second of time shall pass
when to this world
I will not tell
of Your coming.

Take Me and use Me Lord
do as You will through Me,
to help bring a wayward world
to you.
So not one man, not one woman
should be left
when time as we know it
comes to an end.

I'm yours
FOR ALL TIME!!

Inspired By God
Melinda L. Moreland
November 7, 2000

Melinda L. Moreland

HEALING

Beginning of life
a father, a daughter
a love that could
not be tarnished.
But it was.

Somewhere down the road
a love so cherished
nothing could tear
at its heart.
Yet it did.

Finally turning to Him
a child's heart healed
a woman's spirit touched
forgiveness intact
love renewed
Jesus did it.

Inspired By God
Melinda L. Moreland
November 15, 2000

LOVING HANDS

So much heartache today
in a world so lost.
Hurting the ones you love
the ones you can't live without
at what cost.

It is not them
that has turned your tide.
It is your own heart
you cannot abide.

Love your family,
love your friends,
love the people of
this world no matter what,
and your broken heart
lay in My hands.

You cannot heal a million
heartaches but I can,
You cannot throw the anger
away but I can.
I can mend all the wounds.
Trust me, sleep and be at peace
while in your place
I STAND!!!

Inspired By God
Melinda L. Moreland
November 17, 2000

Melinda L. Moreland

HAVE FAITH IN ME

So lost and alone
feeling like the world's
against you.
Come to me
Grow in faith.

You wake in the morning
your husband is angry
once again.
Come to me
Grow in faith.

You lose your home,
you lose your family
you lose it all
but do you?
Come to me
Walk in faith.

Inspired By God
Melinda L. Moreland
November 19, 2000

LOOK FOR THE ANSWERS

A day will come
when all that crosses your heart
is a prayer for death.

A day will come
when your only desire
will be for mercy.

How sad your
life has come to that.
When God was and is
the answer to what
eternity holds.

Don't be left
when Jesus parts the sky.
Fore the map to Heaven
is found on your knees.
For in His Presence
you will be.

Inspired By God
Melinda L. Moreland
November 25, 2000

Melinda L. Moreland

NO WORRIES

A world so lost, feeling alone.
Not knowing what
tomorrow may hold.
Wondering and waiting
while living in limbo.

A King standing in the shadows.
Wondering when you'll
turn to Him.
For the answers you seek.

Destiny and salvation
alone to Him give .
for your yesterday,
today, and tomorrow
have always been His.

Inspired By God
Melinda L. Moreland
November 30, 2000

THE CHOICE IS YOURS

You cannot heal a wound
without the right
medicine.

You cannot give a child
a smile.
Without a smile
in your heart.

You cannot love
a stranger
If yourself you hate
the most.

You cannot lead
a man
to God if in your soul
God's not allowed.

You're not living
if to Him your hearts
Not been given.

The choice is yours
today to stand.
Stand…

Inspired By God
Melinda L. Moreland
November 30, 2000

Melinda L. Moreland

MOTHER

A little girl
sometimes feeling lost
sometimes feeling alone.
A mother holding her
in loving arms.

A little girl
sometimes scared
needing a place to hide.
Her mother's arms
are always there.

A little girl
who's grown into a woman
not always knowing
what tomorrow holds.
Yet sure her mother's arms
are still loving.

Thank you Lord
for my mother
and her loving arms.

Inspired By God
Melinda L. Moreland
December 1, 2000

Dedicated to my Mom Donna Montoya

YOUR FORGIVEN

Rose petals so soft
and fragile to the touch.
Yet they can give
you joy or break a heart.

Dew in the soft morning
lightly wetting the leaves.
So beautiful it can
touch our hearts
if we take a moment to see.

It just took a moment
in a garden alone.
Jesus
waiting and knowing
what the sunrise
would bring.
His life given,
Yours forgiven.

Inspired By God
Melinda l. Moreland
December 1, 2000

Melinda L. Moreland

WHERE HAS ALL THE LOVE GONE

A women beaten so badly
she wonders if tomorrow will come.
She wonders if she cares.
In Heaven Jesus cries
Where has all the love gone?

A child hiding in his room
feeling like no one wants him
thinking no one cares.
While his parents sit in another room
not knowing or caring that he is there.
In Heaven Jesus cries
Where has all the love gone?

A girl who's turned into a woman
too fast now a mother she
must be or maybe not.
She's not sure where to
turn every one who says
they love her, lives in a world that
has no time for anyone else.
In Heaven Jesus cries
Where has all the love gone?

WHERE HAS ALL YOUR LOVE GONE?

Inspired By God
Melinda L. Moreland
December 2, 2000

WALK FREE

A life so torn
between right and wrong,
life and death.
Yet in dark hours
Jesus is where you turn.

A soul who knows Him
and wants to live for Him
Yet the call of the world
seems louder, and easier to find.

One day soon you
will find eternity is waiting
and there's not much time

So what if you have
few tomorrow's or none.
If eternity with Him
is where you'll stand.

Just Believe
Walk Free..

Inspired By God
Melinda L. Moreland
December 3, 2000

Melinda L. Moreland

JUST ASK HIM

A child sleeping
peacefully, while
the world carries on
around him.
Because Jesus holds him
while he sleeps.

A family praying
quietly in a room
filled with the spirit and
love of Jesus.
Because Jesus was asked
to be there.

A man walking through
his home, as all sleep
touching each door, and each love.
Asking Jesus in.
That's where Jesus begins.
Just ask Him in..

Inspired By God
Melinda L. Moreland
December 3,2000

WHAT BECOMES

What becomes of the unborn
child so casually thrown away?
Only Jesus holds the answer
to this question.

What becomes of a family
God put together
yet this world so
viciously tore apart..
Only God holds the answer
to this question.

What becomes of a world
walking in sin and shame?

Jesus Comes.
All is known.

Inspired By God
Melinda L. Moreland
December 12, 2000

Melinda L. Moreland

A FATHER, A FRIEND, A UNCLE AN ANGEL TO THE END

A child so small following a man
whose heart was strong.
A guardian angel with comforting arms,
always standing tall.
Jesus saw the man.

Many years have passed,
many days gone by.
The man still good
the heart still strong.
Even better now since to Jesus
it belongs.
Jesus always saw the man.

Heaven bound the man now is
on the wings of a hawk.
who in a tree waited
for the man's journey to start.

No worries, no pain,
no sorrow is left
for in His bosom Juke
Now rest.

Inspired By God
Melinda L. Moreland
December 15, 2000

Dedicated to Diana Sandoval

Cherish ME

LAST CHANCE

Days traveling on
at such a fast pace.
The saints just waiting
not entering the worlds race.

The saints they pray to
the Lord up above
daily to him they speak,
a friend He has become.

A day will come to
them that wait,
to them that pray to
Him each day.
When Jesus comes and
takes them away.

Yet on this earth how sad to say
some loved ones will have to stay.
Fore when the chance was
given to them they thought they
still had one more day to wait.

Now in the time
that they have left
their souls to Him must
be given.
LAST CHANCE

Inspired By God
Melinda L. Moreland
December 16, 2000

Melinda L. Moreland

FEEL HIS PEACE

Music softly drifting
through my mind as
I sit thinking of
Jesus and what he
means to my heart.

In His presence
I go to the mountains.
In Heaven I sit in
the meadows and have
quiet moments with
God, and let His
love just walk me
through this life of mine.

So peaceful His spirit is
When turmoil arises
His love steps in
mending our souls,
touching our hearts,
and healing our pain.

Just sit back and relax
let Jesus reign
in your heart for all time.

Inspired By God
Melinda L. Moreland
December 17, 2000

IF NOT FOR THAT NIGHT

If not for that night,
When to this earth,
In a stable God did
send His Son
Jesus
Where would we be?

If not for that night,
Jesus would not have
hung on a tree
for our sins forgiven.
Where would we be?

If not for that night,
There would be no hope
for what tomorrow
might bring.
Where would we be?

Lost without any hope
for salvation.
YET
Jesus was Born
Jesus Died
Jesus Lives
Jesus is coming soon for
His children.
Hope!!!!

Inspired By God
Melinda L. Moreland
December 17, 2000

Melinda L. Moreland

A PART OF ONE

They walked together
in this life of their's,
a brother a sister,
friends it would seem
to all who see..
He was part of her
she was part of him

A tragedy of sorts…
no life taken
Yet just as bad their
hearts torn apart.
He took part of her
she took part of him.

Years passing, days
going by, life's in limbo
to them; to the
world they're just fine…
he still has her part
she still has his.

Reaching an age
where there's no turning
back, and time to be
together is running out fast.
He longs for her
She longs for him.
A brother and sister for
them to be again.

So God reaches down
with His wisdom and love
and joins two parts
two hearts in love.

Cherish ME

One brother one sister
apart no more.

Inspired By God
Melinda L. Moreland
December 29, 2000

Dedicated to my brother Rick La Par

Melinda L. Moreland

HEAVEN WAITS

Lost it seems
to all who see
yet Heaven waits
for me for you.

Traveling down roads
that seem to be going
in the wrong direction
yet Heaven waits
for me for you.

Jesus standing
at the gate
arms open wide.
Heaven waits
for me for you.

Inspired By God
Melinda L. Moreland
January 1,2001

Cherish ME

JUST TURN TO HIM

When the world seems
lost heartache nearly
killing you.
When it feels like there
is no love around.
Just turn to Him.

Knife in hand
To your heart held
let the blood flow
to heal a heart
broken beyond
what this world
can understand
Just turn to Him.

When all felt lost
there was a love that
held you tight in the
dark lonely night.
Jesus
Just turn to Him..

Inspired By God
January 3,2001
Melinda L. Moreland

Melinda L. Moreland

HARVEST TIME

A farmer in his fields
gathering his crops.
It's harvest time!

A pastor in his church
gathering his flock.
It's harvest time!

A family in their home
gathering all as one.
It's harvest time!

A SON in the sky
arms wide,
here to gather His
Children.
It's Harvest Time!!!!

Inspired By God
January 7, 2001
Melinda L. Moreland

HOW EASILY

How easily we turn to man
with a problem or
when just sad.

How easily we are touched
by a man who walks alone not
yet knowing of God's love.

How easily we believe
all the tales that
come our way,
never hesitating to repeat
the stories of the day.

Yet with each breath we take,
and each thought we make
we ask Him for a miracle
to be sure that He's not fake.

Inspired By God
January 7, 2001
Melinda L. Moreland

Melinda L. Moreland

WHERE DOES YOUR TRUST LIE

Your children running wild
hearts of man
that belong to no one.
Do you trust Me?
Give them to Me.

Your friend, your life,
has found someone new
what about the
love you feel so lost?
Do you trust Me?
Give it to Me.

Alone, you now
stand in a world
that cares none.
Yet here I am.
Do you trust Me?
Come walk with me then.

Inspired By God
Melinda L.Moreland
January 14, 2001

HE WALKS THERE TO

Climbing a cliff it seems
my soul screams
for a heart full of love
to lead me,
He walks there too,
Carrying me!

Snow falling all around
my body feeling the cold
my heart feeling the
loss of love, I think,
Yet unknown to me
He walks there too,
Carrying me!

Each heart around
feeling this ache
now, maybe then,
not knowing where to turn,
yet turning to Him.
He walks there too,
carrying me,
carrying you!

Inspired By God
January 28, 2001
Melinda L. Moreland

Melinda L. Moreland

I'M STILL THERE

When nothing could
reach your heart
so aching
I was there.

When nothing could
heal a life
so in glory to be
I was there.

When nothing but
My life, My blood
could mend
your wounds
I was there.

to die for you
to live for you
to walk when
you could not
I'm still there.

Inspired By God
February 17, 2001
Melinda l. Moreland

GOD DID

I stand watching as a woman
cries lost it seems,
so long in sin she's been
this world believes not
that her heart could change.
Yet Jesus Did!!

I listen as a man turns to his friend
and tells him of the love he's found
in Jesus arms the friend laughs
knowing what the man has done through his life
he didn't believe the man could change
Yet Jesus Did!!

Our faith it seems
so weak these days
We don't believe a man can change
Yet Jesus Did
On a Cross for you and me!!!!!!

Inspired By God
February 18. 2001
Melinda L. Moreland

Melinda L. Moreland

I'M THERE TO

When you stand hands raised
towards heaven
praise Me!
I stand there with you.

When bowing down
on knees so low
In My Presence you
seek to be
praise Me!
I kneel there with you.

When on your face
looking only towards
the throne
praise Me!
I lay there with you.

Open your hearts,
your spirits to,
and see I'm there
to walk you through
I'm there to…….

Inspired By God
February 25, 2001
Melinda L. Moreland

LONGING FOR HOME

The dawn breaks
upon the mountains
as it does each time
for us to welcome.
I long for home.

The sweet smell
of coffee wakes you
softly you think
yet it's in His Presence
you will be.
I long for home.

You hear the children
laugh as a new day
comes alive
In hearts so full
of life, love, and Jesus.
I long for home.

I long for laughter
I long for hope
I long for peace
I long for home
Kneeling at Jesus feet.

Inspired By God
February 26, 2001
Melinda L. Moreland

Melinda L. Moreland

FINALLY HOME

Jesus came,
and home is now where
Gerry rests.
In arms so sweet,
and loving
at last now peace he has.

A father, a grandpa,
a friend, a loved one too.
Now lost to us it seems
yet in heaven he now
waits.

Our hearts are breaking,
and feeling such loss.
yet in Heaven the angels
did sing when through the
gates Gerry did walk,
Into loving arms.

He's finally home

Inspired By God
March 4, 2001
Melinda L. Moreland

Dedicated to my friend Chyrel Doyon Rue

I WISH LORD

Yesterday I sat in
the shadows of my life
needing to hide,
wishing for tomorrow
yet dreading the daylight
of that new day.

I know it's You
I'm reaching for Lord,
but I can't reach
You, it seems.
My heart, my hurts
are buried too deep inside.

I wish for the sunshine
to break through.
I want happiness to
overwhelm me.
I need a life that
doesn't know what pain is.

I wish Lord,
but most of all
I pray Lord,
Heal Me

Inspired By God
Melinda L. Moreland
March 7, 2001

Melinda L. Moreland

STANDING TALL

A woman standing
head bowed
tears gently falling
the world moved on.
Yet
in His arms everything
was still.
While Jesus stood tall.

A small child hiding
under his bed in the dark
he made not a sound
as he cried through
the night.
the world moved on
Yet
in His arms everything
was still.
While Jesus stood tall.

A little girl all alone
looking at her freckled
reflection as the tears
fall across a heart
lost so long ago.
the world moved on.
Yet
in His arms everything
was still.
While Jesus stood tall.

Inspired By God
Melinda L. Moreland
March 26, 2001

THE RAIN

It rained yesterday
My tears were in
that rain.

Tears for the broken
for my children
so lost from the flock.

Yet also there was
love and hope
in those tears.

For the heart that's open,
the willing soul
the searching,
the one standing
willingly at the throne.

While standing in the rain
Let Me touch your soul.

Inspired By God
Melinda L. Moreland
April 1. 2001

Melinda L. Moreland

THE SADNESS

A father sitting at
his child's bedside
he's dying maybe
maybe not.

the father cries out
Lord, please don't
take my child.

The Lord comes to the man
"Why should I not?"
The father cries," because I love him."

The Lord says, "did you show him,
does he know?"
The father answers,
"he doesn't know."

The Lord says,
"do you spend time with him,
do you hold him in
your arms, do you listen to his heart,
do you share yours?"

The father answers, "no."

The Lord replies,
"then why should I leave him?"

A husband, a wife, a mother,
or friend
the sadness is the same
it seems to the end.

Are we too hardened

Cherish ME

    to love like Him
      On A Cross
   Arms Open wide..

WHY DID HE STAY?

Inspired By God
Melinda L. Moreland
   April 1, 2001

Melinda L. Moreland

LOOK TO YOUR HEARTS

Standing in the shadows
of a world that cares no more.
Looking and searching for My Light.
Yet I am not far you will find.
Look to your hearts,
I dwell there.

Children walking
in the dark finding not
the love that they should be given.
Lost at every turn, it seems
"What can we say," a whisper says.
Look to your hearts,
I dwell there.

Why do you keep searching and
searching for a love that's
true, when all you have to do is look
inside you?
Look to your hearts,
I DWELL THERE!!!

Inspired By God
April 22, 2001
Melinda L. Moreland

EVOLUTION OF PRAYER TO FAITH

THE BEGINNING:
Please Lord, please Lord,
please Lord, are you listening
to me. Oh, please Lord.

DOWN THE ROAD:
OK, Lord, here I am again.
Lord, I need some help.
Can you take care of this for me?
Wait, I think I've figured out the answer.
No, maybe you better handle it.
I got it now.

GOT IT RIGHT:
Here's what the deal is, Lord.
Thanks for taking care of it.
I Love You!!!!!
WHEN ARE WE GONNA GET IT RIGHT?

Inspired By God
April 29, 2001
Melinda L. Moreland

Melinda L. Moreland

SO LOST

I pray for you
each day my friend.
So sad it seems you've
lost your way.

Trying to answer
all your questions with
yesterdays.
When tomorrow holds
all you need.

You've thrown all
that matters,
your life, your loves
into the wind.
Who's left weeping in the end?

Turn to Jesus, now is the time
He is the only one
who can turn the tide of the
ocean you are in,
and send you home again.

Inspired By God
May 1, 2001
Melinda L. Moreland

IN MY TIME

Standing in the shadows
peeking out from the clouds
around your heart.
God, are you there?
have you answered my prayer?
IN MY TIME.

Climbing the mountain
not knowing if that
next mile will find me
finally home.
Lord, are you going to answer
my prayer?
IN MY TIME.

The dawn breaks early,
rising in the east.
Like a flash of lighting
in the sky He stands,
the trumpets sound.
IT'S MY TIME.

Inspired By God
May 7, 2001
Melinda L. Moreland

Melinda L. Moreland

A TEACHER'S LOVE

God Said: "I give you
this teacher to teach,
nourish, and love your children
when away from you they be."

God Said: See her,
how filled with love can
one person be, as she
lovingly wipes a nose,
pats a head, or holds
a child, maybe yours.

God Said: "What will tomorrow
hold for this child so loved
at home, yet so loved by
a teacher's love?"

God Says: "A life, A future,
love, HEAVEN."

Take a moment,
take a life time if you need
to tell that special teacher
what she's given; how she's
touched your life.

THANK YOU!!!!

Inspired By God
Melinda L. Moreland
May 8, 2001

Dedicated to Mrs. Morag Hunt

Cherish ME

TEACHER

She stand's looking out towards the sea.
She wonder's.
A small child walks up behind her,
takes her hand,
looks at her lovingly,
and smiles.

It's early, another day beginning
children not listening,
crying, and playing when there's
things to get done.
She wonders.
The small child standing beside
brushes her arm ever so gently,
"I Love you," she say's.

A million children,
a million days
passing ever so gently as
if on a wave.
She wonders,
Has it all been worth it.

Listen to the laughter
as they play.
Listen to there hearts when
they look at you and say,
"I Love You Teacher,
Thank You For Today."

Inspired By God
Melinda L. Moreland
May 11, 2001

Dedicated to Ms. Sue Martin

Melinda L. Moreland

SO BLESSED AM I

Joseph, I see the sun rise
in your eyes and
I feel the warmth
of a summer morning
in your heart.
So blessed am I to
have you for a child.

Dawna, my little angel
from above the world
watches as your eyes
change like the leaves
of autumn, and in your
arms life is like spring.
So blessed am I to
have you for a child.

Each one so unique in
your own way.
So blessed am I
that God chose me for
your mom.

Inspired By God
May 15, 2001
Melinda L. Moreland

Dedicated to Joseph & Dawna Mama loves you

OR JESUS

What does tomorrow hold
when your heart has been
broken.
A life full of yesterday's,
or Jesus

What does tomorrow hold
when your children have
gone their own way, and your
love to it seems.
A life time of sorrows,
or Jesus

Tomorrow will always be
tomorrow, and yesterday
just left behind.
What will they hold for you
brokenness and sorrow?
Or life-
JESUS..

Inspired By God
May 19, 2001
Melinda L. Moreland

Melinda L. Moreland

HE CARES

A child's smile, the laughter
that could tear a heart
out with joy. thrown in
the wind so casually.
No one cares.

A family lost in
the shuffle of this world,
torn apart, yet still loving.
Is there anyone out there
who still cares?

Each walking
so quietly to the alter.
Where hope still lives.
He cares.

Inspired By God
May 20, 2001
Melinda L. Moreland

WHEN

So many broken hearts,
so many lost, not knowing where
to turn. We show no
love, we show them not the
Son of Man. Yet the compassion
of a world who cares not.

Where does your heart lie?
When do you show him to a
hurt world? When it's too late,
when the wrist has been cut,
when there is nothing but
tears and brokenness left?

Yesterday's tears, tomorrow sorrows;
when do you bring Jesus in?
When is someone good enough for your time?
For you to spend a moment
in prayer for the mother, father, and
child who stand hurting?
Don't throw away any more tomorrow
when today Jesus here stands.

Inspired By God
Melinda L. Moreland
June 3, 2001

Melinda L. Moreland

A FATHERS DAY

So early he leaves off to
work he must go. Each step he
takes is full of love,
for the ones he left sleeping
in the early dawn.

His hands are so strong
from his labors of love
they hold his children tight
when they need a hug.

Sometimes he is grumpy,
sometimes he is tired,
sometimes he may be just too
busy for them it may seem.

Yet in his heart that
beats so strong.
there lives a man whose
the child of a King.
Yet a father to me.

Inspired By God
May 17, 2001
Melinda L. Moreland

Dedicated to Roy, A Wonderful Husband and Father
From Me, Joe & D. J.

WAITING

As the shadows gently fall across
the aspens, she walks quietly
looking for something.
What?
Jesus stands in the shadows
waiting.

Questions with no answers
nagging at her heart.
Where does she turn
when tomorrow starts.
Why can't life be as
peaceful as this moment she wonders.
Jesus stands in the shadows
waiting.

When she was young there seemed
to always be something new
around the corner. Now life
seems lost with nothing to hope for.
Jesus stands in the shadows
waiting.

She enters the meadow, wonders if child hood
prayers can refresh a spirit
that is no longer new.
She kneels, heart towards heaven.
Jesus steps from the shadows.

Inspired By God
May 19, 2001
Melinda L. Moreland

Melinda L. Moreland

HER HEART CRIES

She stands with her
children alone.
she wonders,
What the next day will hold.

The child reaches
for his mom,
I'm hungry.
She takes his hand
I know baby.
Her heart cries.

The child comes
to her mom crawls in her lap
I'm cold.
She holds her in
her arms.
Her heart cries.

At night she lies in
her bed alone,
Tears falling freely.
She prays please God
make everything O.K.

They've been
left behind so he can go on.
Each one so alone,
Each one needing comfort,
needing love.
Her heart cries.

Jesus touches the heart
as only he can..
He reaches down,

Cherish ME

and holds the mother close
touching her, giving her heart comfort.

Tomorrow in this world
may be the same. Except Jesus now holds the tissue
to wipe her tears. Her heart cries no more.

Inspired By God
Melinda L. Moreland
June 24, 2001

Dedicated to my sister Kim La Par

Melinda L. Moreland

A HEARTFELT PRAYER

THE PRAYER
WILL YOU GO
BELIEVE
FOR YOU
I'M HERE
ONE TEARDROP TO MANY
THE DREAM
I LOVE YOU
WONDER
PEACE
PREPARE
BEGINNING
I HEAR
TAKE THE TIME
GOD'S LOVE
SUFFER THE LITTLE CHILDREN
ARE YOU
HE CAN
OK LORD
HERE I STAND
STEP FROM THE BOAT
HANNAH ANGEL
HE'S THERE
SOMETHING SO SIMPLE
NOT EVEN A THOUGHT
SPECIAL MOMENTS
DEAR GOD
JUST LISTEN
WALK WITH ME
THE TIME HAS COME FOLLOW ME
THE CHILD
I AM SPEAKING
AS IT SHOULD BE
JUST AS
COME LIVE WITH ME

Cherish ME

MAKE THE CHOICE
ALL I AM
GO ALL THE WAY
TURN TO ME
THAT'S WHO JESUS IS
JUST LET JESUS
HOW JESUS MUST LOVE US
TIME
A LOVE GIVEN
TOUCH A HEART
JESUS IS COMING
DO IT NOW
IN DUE TIME
WHAT WOULD YOU DO

Melinda L. Moreland

A MOTHER'S PRAYER

WHAT MORE DO WE NEED
JUST A MATTER OF TIME
HOME TIME
FOR ALL TIME
HEALING
LOVING HANDS
HAVE FAITH IN ME
LOOK FOR THE ANSWERS
NO WORRIES
THE CHOICE IS YOURS
MOTHER
YOUR FORGIVEN
WHERE HAS ALL THE LOVE GONE
WALK FREE
JUST ASK HIM
WHAT BECOMES
A FATHER, A FRIEND, A UNCLE
LAST CHANCE
FEEL HIS PEACE
IF NOT FOR THAT NIGHT
A PART OF ONE
HEAVEN WAITS
JUST TURN TO HIM
HARVEST TIME
HOW EASILY
WHERE DOES YOUR TRUST LIE
HE WALKS THERE TO
I'M STILL THERE
GOD DID
I'M THERE TO
LONGING FOR HOME
FINALLY HOME
I WISH LORD
STANDING TALL
THE RAIN

Cherish ME

THE SADNESS
LOOK TO YOUR HEARTS
EVOLUTION OF PRAYER TO FAITH
SO LOST
IN MY TIME
A TEACHER'S LOVE
TEACHER
SO BLESSED AM I
OR JESUS
HE CARES
WHEN
A FATHER'S DAY
WAITING
HER HEART CRIES

Melinda L. Moreland